Lifted

Given a New Song to Sing

by Katie Payne

DARE 2 SHARE

A D2S Publishing book
PO Box 745323
Arvada, CO 80006

Editor: Jane Dratz

Payne, Katie
Lifted: Given a New Song to Sing
ISBN: 978-0-9857352-5-8
Library of Congress Control Number: 2013947996

Printed in the United States of America
1 2 3 4 5 6 7 8 9 / 14 13 12 11 10 09 08

This is for the ones who are looking
for hope, for love, or a future.
This is written for you.
Your story's not over.

He lifted me out of the pit of despair,
out of the mud and the mire...
He has given me a new song to sing.

Psalm 40:2-3

Prologue

Usually, the prologue is the place where the author (me), is supposed to tell the reader (you), all about his/her credentials, intellect and skills, and why they are qualified to write a book.

But here's the thing… I'm not qualified.

I don't have a college degree.

I don't have a stellar resume.

I'm not anyone really that influential.

I'm just some random, 18-year-old kid from Illinois.

I'm really not anyone special on my own.

That's the thing, really. This book isn't actually about me. It's about God. I just get to play a part in His big story.

For years I ran away from Him, trying to make sense of things by myself. I couldn't. I found myself in a lot of trouble because of my pigheadedness. But I'm standing here today because God loved me too much to let me continue on my own way. And I'm writing to you today because I want to let you know God loves you too much to let you continue on your own way.

I'm not a prodigy. I'm a prodigal. I'm not qualified, but neither were many of the young people in the Bible that God chose to use—like Gideon, David or Peter.

I'm telling you God's story, lived out through me. I'm telling you about the collision between the holy and the haggard. I'm relaying how a dead person came back to life, lifted out of the pit of despair and put on a new road of hope.

But I should probably start at the beginning.

Shattered Innocence

I wish I could begin my story with a "Once upon a time, in a land far away…"

I wish I could say my story began with a celestial premonition or a godmother's gift.

But no. My story is far from a fairy tale. Mine is the all-too-common story of innocence ripped away. Filled with pain and doubt and struggle. And with redemption.

It started out ordinary enough. I was born to ordinary parents. My dad had an ordinary job, and my mom stayed at home to take care of me.

I learned to crawl, talk, and walk. For three years, it was just my parents and me. Then I got a little brother. I also started preschool around that time.

My mom taught me the alphabet; I quickly found I loved to read. Soon I was reading the *Magic Tree House* series and *Junie B. Jones*. Every night Dad would come home, and I would hide behind the curtains for him to find me. He would thank Mom for dinner, and we would sit down and eat together as a family.

When I was four, my dad got a new job. He proved to be really good at it, and quickly moved up the corporate ladder. He started spending more time at work, and less time with us. He began coming home stressed and short tempered. He stopped playing hide and seek with me. He would grunt at dinner, and would head back to his bedroom to watch TV.

I think that was when things started getting hard. Mom was always strong willed, and she had little patience for Dad's attitude. Most nights she would either seethe over dinner while he sat in another room, or she would follow him and throw down the gauntlet.

It wasn't always like this. Not every night. On the weekends, we would take drives and go to the zoo and have picnics and be happy. But when Dad went back to work, we went back to the old pattern. We had good times, but we also had bad times. It was a mix of both.

I don't remember doing a lot of church when I

was young. I mean, we went to the Sunday morning service for a little while, but that was it. My parents' faith wasn't displayed throughout the week, and we didn't make a big deal about God in our house.

When I was five, I started kindergarten. It wasn't the best experience for me. As I mentioned earlier, I already knew how to read, and when the teacher found out, I became the teacher's pet. The other kids caught on, and began bullying me as compensation—if I had the teacher's good attention, then I could have their bad attention.

Initially, I'd had two friends—a boy (so I couldn't really play with him, since everyone knew that boys had cooties) and a girl, who would drop me the instant the bullies told her to. So it wasn't long before I was spending recess alone with my nose in a book, instead of playing with the other kids.

It was a rough year, but eventually kindergarten passed, and I moved on expectantly to first grade. But the emotional distress was the same. Despite the grade change and a new teacher, the kids were still mean and excluded me on every level.

I felt isolated and rejected, making me a vulnerable target when a man came along who offered me special attention.

"Hey, sweetie, are you okay? Why aren't you off playing with your friends?" he asked me one day.

*I felt **isolated** and **rejected**, making me a vulnerable target.*

In the blunt honesty only a six year old can possess, I answered him, "I don't have any friends. All the kids are mean to me."

He stayed silent for a minute before proceeding. "You don't have any friends?"

"No, no one likes me."

"Well, I like you.

It started with him just being my friend, telling me stories and talking to me about things that interested him. He told me about history. He told me about ancient Egyptians, and how they enslaved the Hebrews to build the pyramids. He told me about pirates, and how they sailed back and forth across the ocean. About King Arthur and the Knights of the Round Table. About friends and enemies and wars and peace and everything in between. He wove words together in a tapestry.

I began trusting him. When someone would make fun of me, I would confide in him. When my parents would have a particularly bad fight, he would listen. And when I felt lonely, he always had a story ready.

He made me feel special. Sometimes he would pull me onto his lap as we would talk. He would give me little things—little dollar beanie babies, a flower, stickers for my folder, trinkets that might make me smile. And every time I smiled, he would tell me, "That's what I've been waiting for!"

And he would laugh and give me a hug.

And I would be happy.

He warned me not to tell anyone that he was spending time alone with me. He would wink at me and say that it would be "our little secret."

I trusted him; he wouldn't let me get in trouble. One day, he looked at me with a strange brightness in his eyes and said, "Katie, I have a special surprise for you today. But it's too big to carry out here. Would you come with me and see it?" He smiled like he had a great present for me, grabbed my hand and led me away.

He stopped in front of a large, foreboding door. He pulled out a key from his pocket, pushed it into the lock, and jangled and turned it until the door clicked. He leaned into the door and slowly opened it.

"Is this your office?" I asked him as I walked into

the small space. It had a small table in the corner with a moth eaten swivel chair. Metal cabinets stood next to the door. The whole space was only about twelve square feet. There was a bigger open space in the middle of the floor. Various supplies stood like soldiers around the perimeter of the little room.

Once we were alone in this private space, he looked at me silently for a moment before getting on his knees in front of me. "Katie, this will be our little secret, right? And we've gotta be really quiet, okay?" I nodded silently. My mind raced; what could he possibly be talking about? He said he had a big surprise for me. I had told him the week before about a book that I had wanted to read. Could it be that? Or maybe he had made me something himself. That would be cool.

"Katie, I need you to close your eyes."

I eagerly consented. I didn't suspect what happened next.

Rough hands grabbed my shoulders. Pushed me down onto the floor. Elbows held my chest down, and I felt my clothes being removed. I couldn't open my eyes; I was too scared.

What was happening?

An arm lay across my chest. A hand covered my mouth. Hot breath was on my cheek, in my ear.

What was going on?

Hot, heavy tears came. I couldn't breathe, and I tried to push him off. I felt dirty. Blood pounded in my ears. I inhaled quickly, shallowly. I stopped trying to fight. I didn't know how to react.

Then it was over. Hands came off of me. He pushed himself up. Stepped back. Stood up over me. Helped me up. He looked at me and smiled. Winked.

"Our little secret, sweetheart."

I looked to the floor. I nodded. Our little secret.

———————————————

This continued. Not every day, but many days. He knew how to get me alone, and used that to his advantage.

No one could know, because he had said this was to be "our little secret." If he didn't want anyone to know about what he was doing to me, it must be because he was protecting me.

I didn't want to cause problems for the grownups, lest they get angry with me. I wanted to be the good, obedient little girl, so that others would be happy with me. If I told, someone wouldn't have been happy and I thought I would get in trouble. So I stayed quiet.

I took the blame upon myself. When I was hurting, I assumed it was because I wasn't strong enough or smart enough or because something was wrong with me. I wanted to make my friend happy, so I surrendered without a fuss and just stayed quiet.

I trusted this man because I thought he truly was my friend. But he broke that trust.

Eventually, circumstances changed and he moved out of my life. But the hurt he'd inflicted stayed with me.

It's still something I'm working through—I'm still dealing with the fallout of this man's choices. I've had to learn to recognize that this wasn't my fault. What he did, those were HIS decisions, not mine. But back when I was a child, I believed that I was responsible. I didn't realize that I was the innocent victim of an adult with evil intent, and so I took the blame upon myself. Truth is, I was deeply wounded. It affected every part of who I was.

And I don't care who you are, everyone has been hurt by someone about whom they cared deeply. And these kinds of wounds last for a long time.

Maybe you were hurt by someone you trusted, like I was.

Maybe you were hurt by a classmate who made fun of you.

Maybe you were hurt by your parents, who got a divorce.

Maybe you were hurt by society, telling you that you weren't smart enough, pretty enough, fun enough, good enough.

Hurt happens a lot. It's tempting to try and diminish the pain. You say, "At least I'm not starving, or at least I'm not living in poverty," and you try and ignore the hurt you're feeling now. But your pain is real, too. Your hurts matter to God.

*God is a **compassionate** God. And when He sees you hurting... He hurts **WITH** you and **FOR** you.*

God is a compassionate God. And when He sees you hurting, even if it's over a bad grade or a rough breakup, He hurts WITH you and FOR you.

Hebrews 4:14-16 says this:

> *Now that we know what we have—Jesus, this great High Priest with ready access to God—let's not let it slip through our fingers. We don't have a priest who is out of touch with our reality. He's been through weakness and testing, experienced it all—all but the sin. So*

> *let's walk right up to him and get what he is so*
> *ready to give. Take the mercy, accept the help.*
> *(The Message)*

This means that Jesus knows what it's like to feel hurt. He knows what both emotional pain and physical pain feels like—and that means that He can comfort us and love up on us in the middle of all our hurts. He cares so, so much for you. He wants to help you, and He has a big plan for you in the midst of all the bad.

It may be hard for you to see that now in the middle of your hurt. It's still sometimes hard for me to see that truth when I reflect back on what happened.

There's a well-known Bible verse in Romans 8 that a lot of people pull out and unfortunately sometimes use as a kind of band-aid to try to patch things over when something really painful is going on in life. But if you read to the end of this book, I'm hoping that this Bible verse will begin to make more sense to you. The verse is Romans 8:28, and it talks about how God can take everything that happens, and use it for the good of those who love Him. That means everything—both the good and the bad. The things that we can control, and the things that we can't.

It's a sometimes painful, sometimes beautiful truth that God is big enough to redeem *everything* in our lives.

A Backpack Full
of Guilt and Shame

My mind never healed from what happened to me at the hands of that man. I held it inside me, and it began eating away at my heart like an acid. I felt dirty—I carried guilt and shame around like a backpack, and I knew that if anyone ever found out about what happened to me, they would surely hate me. To my reckoning, the whole ordeal was my fault anyway. If I hadn't been nice to him, if I hadn't talked to him, if I had told someone, just done something different, then it wouldn't have happened to me.

My interpretation of those events left me feeling like I was always doing something… wrong. I felt guilty, ashamed and on edge all the time, and I didn't know how to deal with things. I shut down for the most part. I was letting my shame become my identity.

What I needed was a different way of thinking, like what Romans 12:2 talks about when it says: *"Let God transform you into a new person by changing the way you think."* Instead of me telling myself, "I'm stupid, I'm ugly, I'm worthless," God wanted to replace those internal messages with, "I'm precious, I'm beautiful, I'm valuable."

But, I didn't know this then. So instead, I withdrew into my hurting, isolated shell. I found that I could cope as long as I just made life a cycle of school, weekends, family vacations, and trying to make it to the next day. During this time, I got another brother in the mix, but besides that nothing too exciting happened. In all honesty, I don't remember a whole terribly lot from this part of my life. I was just trying to make it through, so I built up walls and put on masks and tried to smile.

But then middle school hit and my pain intensified.

I'm sure you remember your first day of middle school? It was terrifying. Right?

Yeah, mine was too. I was in an entirely new school, and the way the districts were divided I was the only person in my class that had been attending the elementary school I'd gone to. I literally knew no one and had no friends.

So let's take a look at my attributes at this point:

I looked like a nerd with my glasses and books.

I was shy.

I was heavier set.

I was not a Victoria's Secret angel.

I barely talked.

And to top it all off—I looked far older than a 12-year-old.

I was just a bundle of awkwardness.

You remember those days?

So the kids in my class soon began teasing me again. Oodles of fun—or, not so much.

Every day I was reminded of how messed up I was.

"Fat."

"Ugly."

"Nerd."

Twelve-year-olds can be really mean. They mocked me, telling me that I was basically useless and worthless. How I shouldn't be alive. How no one would ever love me. (Because middle schoolers are the ultimate authority on romantic advice. NOT!)

They would laugh at me, tease me, and I would sit and take it. I didn't think I deserved any different.

In the mix of all this, I had a small group of friends. We were all bullied, pretty much. We tried to make each other feel better, but that was like the blind leading the blind. Right off a cliff.

Every night when I would go home, the taunting would still echo in my ears. My mom had started experimenting with God, and as such, she stopped outwardly fighting with Dad. But that didn't mean the tension had dissolved. It was still there. An intangible, yet very real presence.

*Every day I was **reminded** of how **messed up** I was.*

Satan has a strange way of taking one bad feeling, and multiplying it into a thousand lies.

All of my pent up emotions began hitting me at once—what happened when I was a kid, the bullying at school, and the strain between my parents. And because the common denominator was me, I took that to mean that I was the cause of it all.

Which made me feel guilty.

Which made me think I had to pay for it all.

I had to pay for causing the fighting. I had to pay for what happened when I was a kid. I had to pay for being fat. I had to pay for being ugly. I had to pay for being shy. I had to pay for being a loser. I had to pay for being different from everyone else.

The taunting of my classmates turned into voices in my head, following my every step. Every time I stopped and breathed, I would hear echoes of Satan's lies: "Fat, ugly, worthless, you should die now, you should just give up." So I began self-harming in the sixth grade.

I cut to quiet the voices down.

Pain became my addiction.

It was the only way I could feel in control.

And then it became the only way I could feel anything at all.

It didn't begin as an addiction. Nothing ever does. Like so many addictive behaviors, self-harm begins by making a promise that it can't deliver on. It promises peace and escape. It says, "Let me help you feel better." But no matter how frequently or intensely someone engages in any addictive behavior, that "help" is always just out of reach. So you do it again, and again, trying to get that "high." But it never lasts.

For two long years I spiraled further and further down this hole.

My little circle of friends, whom I had kept for the entirety of sixth and seventh grade, had no clue. I learned to put a happy face on for them, and pretend that I still felt alive.

Pain became my addiction.

But I was dying inside.

By the time I was in seventh grade, I was sick of everything. The voices in my head were relentless. They never quieted down. I needed an escape. I began planning my own suicide at this point. I never wanted to die. I only wanted to stop hurting. Death would just be a side effect.

I was sick of that feeling. That feeling of never being good enough, never being worth anything, never having hope.

To one degree or another, I think we all know that feeling. How it feels to be abandoned, to be forgotten, to be ridiculed. We all know how much it hurts.

If you're struggling with that now, or if you have in the past, I'm here to tell you to hang on. I don't know if you're contemplating suicide right now, or if that's even a thought on the horizon. But I'm here to tell you to keep going. Fight. Talk to someone you trust. Share with them the details of your story, let them help you find the help you need. You can't do this alone. That's why God is here.

One Foot Over the Edge

This is where I can really see God working. We've established that, at 13 years of age, I was in the deepest, darkest place that I had ever been in. I was standing at the precipice of a sixty story building, and had one foot over the edge. But God has a way of reaching into the darkness to save the day in the nick of time.

When I was six, we had stopped going to church. All talk of God had really stopped in our house. As a family, we were pretty indifferent. Mom and Dad still fought a lot, but they had been raised in church and divorce, in their eyes, wasn't an option. For years we left Christians alone. I didn't go to church, didn't grow up going to church, and I was fine with it.

But like I said earlier, by the time I was in middle

school my mom had was starting to really pursue God more passionately. For a while, she mostly kept it to herself, until I found my life unraveling. Then she started getting bold in her faith.

I don't know how, or if, she knew specifically what was going on with me, but I imagine some part of her intuitively knew something was up. She pulled me out of school during my seventh grade year so that she could teach me at home.

She began talking to me about this God she had found. But it was my mom. And as a middle schooler, I wasn't going to listen to anything she had to say.

God has a way of reaching into the darkness to save the day in the nick of time.

I was angry at her, I was angry at God, and I was angry at basically everything else.

That didn't stop her, though. She decided that I had to stop contact with my old friends, and I had to start going to the church that she was attending.

Looking back, I see how wise that was, and I thank her for that. But at the time I was more put out than a hipster who hears their favorite band on mainstream radio.

Still, I obeyed her.

When I'm Feeling **Angry** at God, I Think About This...

In my experience, when I'm feeling angry at God, it's often because I'm hurt and confused about what's going on in my life. Or sometimes I'm just plain angry at God because I'm upset about an injustice that happened in the past. I question God's goodness and His plans for my future. I wonder how He could possibly redeem the difficult things in my life.

Here are some Bible verses that have spoken to me in the midst of those kinds of feelings. Sometimes it helps to be reminded that these promises are true, so I can cling to them in my confusion and anger.

- God sees my problems, and He's going to defend me. **Psalm 10:14-15**

- God hears my prayers. **Psalm 28:6**

- God is good. **Psalm 34:8**

- God bears my burdens with me. **Psalm 68:19**

- God is coming to strengthen me. **Isaiah 43:4**

- God will bring me justice. **Isaiah 46:13**

- God is doing everything to do well by me. **Jeremiah 29:11-13**

- God hears me, even when I'm at my lowest. **Lamentations 3:55-57**

- The Holy Spirit helps in my weakness. **Romans 8:26**

- God interweaves everything in my life—both the light and the dark—into something He can use for my good. **Romans 8:28**

- God has immense good in mind for me. **1 Corinthians 2:9**

- God is able to do more than I can possibly imagine. **Ephesians 3:20-21**

It can also help to read some of the stories in the Old Testament about people who went through rough times—like Joseph, Daniel, Ruth, Esther and Job.

So Mom started carting me to this church. She said they had a youth group of kids about my age. The first time I remember meeting them was at a game night sort of thing.

All I remember is thinking, "What on earth is wrong with these kids?"

They were all so happy. And they were just goofing off with each other. Having a good time.

The oldest guy—the youth pastor, he was obviously weird. He was all smiles and was acting like one of the kids. It looked like there was really no separation between him and them. Though later, as I got to know him better, I realized this was a reflection of his great people skills.

Ugh, I thought. This place was so dumb. There was no way that they would like someone like me. Obviously all these kids had grown up in church, and nothing bad had ever happened to them. They were good people. Not like me.

And then they introduced themselves to me! Like. What? Guys. Stop it. You don't want to have anything to do with me.

Oh no, but they did. They included me in the games. And at the end of the night, when they were talking about God, they included me in the discussion.

But I didn't want to talk about God. God didn't want me. So for most of the night I just didn't talk to anyone and kept to myself.

When my mom picked me up at the end of it, she asked how it went. "Fine," I said. So she took me back the following Sunday for Bible study.

*"What on earth is **wrong** with these kids?"*

It became a pattern. Anytime the youth group offered any sort of activity whatsoever, I was taken. All the Bible studies. All the game nights. All the meals. All the go-karting and movie outings. Every. Single. One. And these kids never got normal! They were all so… happy. We would talk freely in the Bible study. And the kids would share when something bad was happening in their life. But they still were happy, despite the hardships they were going through. What was going on here?

Meanwhile, my mom was still at home, talking to me about God. And all the stuff that was going on in youth group gave me questions to ask her. So I began asking.

We would go on hour long drives and I would just drill her about God. I learned a lot during that time, but God still wasn't real to me.

Because the voices in my head—the lies of Satan—had occupied my heart. They so deeply defined me that I was convinced that God didn't want anything to do with me. That He couldn't love me. That He was too good for me.

Then came spring.

A Beautiful Symmetry

Awhile back, the youth pastor had let everyone know that we'd be going to some kind of weekend thingy. Dare 2 Share. So guess who was going. Mom had me signed up before he was done announcing it during Sunday morning church.

I dreaded it. I would have to spend all night with these joyful Jesus freaks. Gag.

As much as I was loath to go, the weekend eventually came. We got to the church Friday afternoon, and I threw my duffel bag in the back of our vehicle. I climbed in with several other people, and we headed on out for our trip to the city.

We reached the conference center, and stood outside the doors for about an hour or so. Here I was, pressed up against all these God people, acting like I was a part of them. The youth pastor was stupid excited. He was moving all around our group, keeping the kids in line, handing out bracelets, joking with the chaperones, being a big dork. Finally the doors opened, and we shuffled inside out of the cold.

There were so many people. Everywhere I looked, there were more people. More kids. All different kinds. Older, younger, taller, shorter. And in every direction I looked, there seemed to be a person holding a "free hugs" sign. (Since when did hugs start costing money?)

Somehow we ended up in the arena and everyone sat down. Music started playing, and everyone stood up. Some band started rocking out, and I sang along with the words on the screen. I looked down the row, and saw a few people with their hands in the air. What were they doing? Soon the music was over, and we could sit down.

The lights dimmed around us as a man got up on the stage. He talked for a while. I can't remember what he said. But he made us laugh with different jokes and stories. He was weird—he got really, REALLY into his stories, jumping around and gesturing. He had a crazy look in his eye. I sincerely hoped he drank decaf.

The night continued on. My mind began to buzz.

All the "voices" in my head went crazy. All I could think about was how I shouldn't be there, how I shouldn't be a part of what was happening, how I shouldn't be attending a dumb Jesus conference. I wondered if I could somehow escape. I couldn't take all the noise ringing in my ears.

Then all of a sudden, the same crazy man stepped back on stage, and for some reason my mind quieted for the first time in months. That caught my attention. God was nudging me.

*That night God got in my face, and **I understood** for the very first time that I was His beloved.*

The crazy, twitchy man began talking. But something was different in the way he was speaking. Earlier he had been talking with a funny, entertaining, amiable spirit. This time, he spoke urgently. He spoke with authority. He spoke like he had something inconceivably important to say.

He looked out at the audience, at me, and told me that God loved me.

I had heard that before, but never so forcefully. God's Holy Spirit was softening my spirit, so I could hear this whole new message. Did God really love me?

He looked out from the stage, and talked about how God loved me so much, and wanted to restore my relationship with Him. God loved me so much that He took everything bad I had ever done and paid for it all. So I didn't have to pay anymore. So I could be reconnected in relationship back to Him.

The man talked about how God bled for me, so I didn't have to anymore.

That Friday night, God got down on my level. Months of wooing and preparation came to a culmination. That night God got in my face, and I understood for the very first time that I was His beloved. I wasn't some mistake to be forgotten. I wasn't an unfortunate existence who had been rejected.

God pressed me against my seat, and forced me to pay attention to Him.

It felt like God was invading the "hell" of my life, and telling the demons who were holding me captive, that He was taking His daughter home.

That night, the preacher man gave everyone an opportunity to be saved by this God who wanted to save. As tears ran down my face, I ran home to my Daddy.

For nearly my whole life, I had been longing to feel loved, wanted. Like I was important, and that I mattered. I ran from person to person, begging for them to approve of me. But no matter who I turned to, I was rejected in some form or fashion.

You know that feeling, don't you? What teenager doesn't? I'm here to tell you confidently that you aren't going to find the acceptance you're looking for outside of Jesus. You're trying to find it in sports, or in clubs, in intellect, in school, with your boyfriend, with your friends, or your parents, or your siblings. You may be trying to find it in yourself. You want to feel alive. But nothing's working.

Listen closely to me: God is waiting for you. God will accept you, just as you are. You don't need to clean up your act or try and fake a smile to ask Jesus to save you.

Jesus could have come to this earth as a prince in a castle. He could have spent all His time in the synagogues with the religious leaders. He could have kept with the status quo and not rocked the boat.

Instead, He came to the world in the middle of poverty. His birth was surrounded with scandal. Instead of sipping tea with the wealthy and well-connected, Jesus broke bread with the beaten and abused. While His teachings offended many of the religious leaders of His day, His invitation to experience a deeper relationship with God attracted those who were yearning for a breath of fresh air.

*God is **waiting** for you. God will accept you, **just as you are**.*

He loved the cheat, the liar, the prostitute, the broken child, the unloved leper. Those that society cast out, He welcomed in.

His whole life, He held His arms open for the weary to find relief. In His death, He stretched out His arms yet again, so that the whole world may find salvation. It's a beautiful symmetry.

If there was just one thing that I could help you understand, it would be to make sure you know precisely how much you are loved. In today's society, it's hard to feel loved. You're always forced to measure yourself against different standards: Am I skinny enough? Am I smart enough? Am I wealthy enough? Am I good enough? And if you don't reach the world's standards, rejection and condemnation await.

With God, it's totally different. While His standard is holiness, He's made a way for us to measure up. To reach His holy standards on your own, you would literally have to be perfect. But you know that you're not perfect. Being "good" won't make the cut either; no one is truly good. Trying to cover up your bad stuff with good deeds is like trying to use grape juice to get mud stains out of a white t-shirt. You know you're not measuring up to God's standards.

Here's the beautiful thing, though! This world doesn't love you—so when you fail to meet its standards, it doesn't care. But God's heart breaks when you break His standard. His love for you is incredibly immense. So instead of just letting you continue along your way, God did something that totally changed the picture.

He couldn't change His standard, so He changed the playing field. God became man so that He could show us what actual perfection looked like, since we couldn't attain it on our own. For 33 years, Jesus walked and talked and loved people, showing people who God really was. However, just showing people what God LOOKED like wasn't enough. People were still breaking commandments and failing to meet the standard. Their rejection of God demanded a punishment. So Jesus became that punishment.

On a cold Thursday night, this Jesus man was arrested for crimes He didn't commit. He was dragged all over Jerusalem. He was beaten to a pulp. He was rejected by men. He was spit on, mocked, and hated. This torture lasted all night into Friday morning. And after the sun rose over the horizon,

Jesus was nailed to a rough cross, having been sentenced to death. He hung there for hours. The wood groaned under the weight of the man. The man groaned under the weight of our sin.

On that cross at Calvary, Jesus took on all the punishment for all the humans who've ever lived—

If You're Feeling **Worthless**, Think About This...

- God Himself created you. **Psalm 119:73**
- God made you to play a special role in furthering His kingdom, and He will hold your hand through it all. **Isaiah 42:6-7**
- God is so desperately in love with you that He's serenading you. He delights in you. **Zephaniah 3:17**
- God loves you with an everlasting love, and He'll continue to love you. **Jeremiah 31:3**
- You were chosen by God from the beginning to help bring His message to the world. **Jeremiah 1:5**
- As a believer, you are God's child now; you need have fear no longer. **Romans 8:15**
- You are a masterpiece, something God Himself is creating. **Ephesians 2:10**
- God calls you His child. **1 John 3:1**

the punishment for breaking God's standards. You, as a person, had every responsibility to pay for your transgressions yourself. But God simply loved you too much to require that. The book of Hebrews tells us that Jesus endured the cross because of *"the joy that was set before Him."* That's you. As Jesus hung bruised and naked, bleeding and suffocating, you were on His mind. He could have gotten off of that piece of wood. He could have saved Himself. But He was too committed to saving you. It wasn't the nails that held Him against the cross—it was His love for you.

You are God's joy. The book of Zephaniah, in chapter 3, talks about how God literally sings over you. He is so excited about you, so proud of you, so madly in love with you that He is singing. He's bragging to all of creation of His beloved. That's you. You are the apple of God's eye.

You may feel like you're unimportant. Like you're easily forgettable. Like you're worthless, or hopeless, or useless. But God says differently. God says that you are precious in His sight, that you are called for a special purpose, that you are unimaginably important. God thought so highly of you that He died a humiliating death, so that you could be brought back into relationship with Him. That's how cherished you are!

God died so that you may have life. He's right

here, offering you a new heart and a clean slate. No more do you have to sit alone in your darkness, stuck in the mud and the mire, waiting for death. Life is being handed to you on a platter! It's waiting. Won't you say yes?

If You're Feeling **Hopeless**, Think About This...

- God can make you a new person. **2 Corinthians 5:17**
- Once Jesus has freed you from your chains, nothing can condemn you. **Romans 8:1-2**
- God can forgive you for all your sins and they'll be no more, He'll make something new. **Isaiah 43:18-19**
- Even though you experience tough times, know that Jesus has conquered sin and death. **John 16:33**
- God's not done with you—you're a masterpiece in progress! **Philippians 1:6**
- God wants to redeem you, and you can be seen as holy in His sight. **Colossians 1:22**
- Not a SINGLE THING can separate you from God's love! Nothing can prevail with God on your side. **Romans 8:31-39**
- You can be forgiven, and given victory over the evil one. **1 John 2:12-14**

Struggling On

I remember that first night at home, when I got back from the weekend thingy. It was late at night, and I still felt fairly giddy from all the Jesus juice I had gotten that weekend. I wanted to be close to God, so I decided that I would never, ever hurt myself again. And I was really good for about a week. But then that urge came back.

I didn't want to do it, but it had a hold over me. I wanted to stop, and I tried. I didn't return to that, but oh! How I wanted to! It was so hard to say no, and I felt like I was failing for even being tempted. I pulled out my Bible, begging for some sort of comfort. Romans 7 was what it opened up to:

> *I realize that I don't have what it takes. I can will it, but I can't **do** it. I decide to do good, but*

> *I don't **really** do it; I decide not to do bad, but then I do it anyway. My decisions, such as they are, don't result in actions. Something has gone wrong deep within me and gets the better of me every time. It happens so regularly that it's predictable. The moment I decide to do good, sin is there to trip me up. I truly delight in God's commands, but it's pretty obvious that not all of me joins in that delight. Parts of me covertly rebel, and just when I least expect it, they take charge. (Romans 7:18-23, The Message)*

Here's the thing, you guys. Even if we're Christians, we're going to screw up. I can't put it any other way—we're human. It's what we do. It's a good thing that when Jesus died for us on the cross, it was for all our sins, including our future ones.

We both know that we don't want to keep messing up. We both know that when we mess up, we feel terrible.

This is Paul. PAUL. The guy wrote more of the New Testament than any other author. He's like THE super-Christian. And this guy had problems fighting his old sinful nature too.

As I read, it was like God was reaching down to me and saying, "You're going to mess up again. But you will never let Me down; you never were holding Me up to begin with. I will uphold you, and I will be with you."

That's what God is promising us. Even if we're Christians, we will still mess up. We will break commandments and break God's heart and run away from Him. But He will never, EVER leave us.

In Romans 8, Paul continues his thoughts from the previous chapter. Here's my paraphrase of what he's saying: Now there is no condemnation for you, if you're in Christ Jesus. Because you belong to Him, the life-giving Spirit has set you free from the power of sin. All the good works in the world couldn't save you because of your sin, so God Himself did what your good works couldn't do. He sent His Son in a body like the ones we sinners have. In that body, God declared an end to sin's control over us by giving His Son as a sacrifice.

He will never, EVER leave you.

All our mistakes, all our dirt and crud and problems, they don't condemn us now. They've already been paid for, so we don't have to keep paying for them. We can't let Satan convince us that we are not loved by God because we're still sinning. That's simply not true.

Now, does that mean that we can KEEP doing whatever it is we want? Keep willfully sinning? No, of course not!

In Romans 6:1-3, Paul says this:

> *So what do we do? Keep on sinning so God can keep on forgiving? I should hope not! If we've left the country where sin is sovereign, how can we still live in our old house there? Or didn't you realize we packed up and left there for good? (The Message)*

Continuing on in sin after being saved is like returning to economy seating after flying first class on an airplane. In economy, we're served pretzels or peanuts, and our seats are so tiny we're stuck practically spooning the guy next to us. In first class, we get treated to hot towels, gourmet meals, spacious seats and the full attention of the flight attendants. Who in their right mind would choose economy class over first class, now that they have the choice?

That's precisely why we have the power and desire to turn away from our sin after we've put our trust in Jesus. When God steps into our lives, we get a free upgrade. God wants us to stop sinning, not because He's a party pooper, but because He wants what's best for us. Chasing things other than God leads to nothing but heartbreak. God wants to keep us from that. So by calling us to a higher lifestyle, God is caring for us.

But it's not only that. Once we become believers

in Jesus, we represent God and His kingdom to a watching world. We choose to live holy lives, because He is holy. We do what's right, because He is righteous. We strive to deal with sin in our lives, because He crushed sin on the cross.

It's hard to stop sinning. But I'm going to tell you a secret: with God, it's possible. No, I'm not saying that we will become perfect this side of heaven. But I'm saying that in the power of Christ, we will be able to leave behind our old way of life in favor of God's way.

*When God steps into our lives, we get a **free upgrade.***

I said earlier that I still struggle with a lot of things; with self-injury, with depression, with trust issues, and so on and so forth. Would it be easier for me to pick up my blades again and have at it? Of course. And in the beginning, I would give in to the temptation more than I would like to admit— sometimes, not even by actually acting on my desires, but by dwelling on them until I couldn't get them out of my head. But when God began working on me, I could tell.

Over time though, I began to see many aspects of

my life begin to change, bit by bit. I began noticing that the lies that had once defined every part of my existence started receding. That's not to say that I don't still struggle, but I now know that God is mightier than anything that I might think about myself.

Even with my family, I've noticed a change. Years ago, we were struggling. But now, as we grow closer

Bible Verses for When You're Struggling With Sin...

- Jesus knows what you're going through. **Hebrews 4:15**
- God will help you endure. **1 Corinthians 10:13**
- God will be with you during the bad times. **Isaiah 43:2**
- God will never fail you or abandon you. **Deuteronomy 31:6**
- Come close to God, and He will come close to you. **James 4:7-8**
- God is able to help you when you're struggling. **Hebrews 2:18**
- God can transform you. **Romans 12:2**

- You're dead to sin. **Romans 6:1-2**
- God is stronger than your sin strongholds. **Romans 7:15-25**
- Pray! **Luke 22:40**
- Having God's Word in your heart will help you battle sin. **Psalm 119:11**
- God can help you stand strong against struggles. **Ephesians 6:10-11**
- God has chosen you as holy. **1 Peter 1:13-16**

and closer to God, we're growing closer and closer to each other, as well. The way God is moving in my family is amazing; we're not perfect, but we have a new peace and we enjoy our time with each other.

And I know the same thing is true for you. God wants to help you, to heal you, to make you who He meant for you to be. It will be hard. Painful, even. But God will carry you through.

Hope

For that first year, I began getting closer to God. I would tell my old school friends about Him, but they didn't want to hear about God. They thought He was stupid, or nonexistent, and that I was stupid for even believing in Him. But I couldn't help myself; I was so in love with Jesus, I couldn't help but talk about Him.

Because of that, a lot of my old friends shut me out. 2 Corinthians 2:15-16 talks about how God is a sweet aroma to those who are living, but is the smell of death to those who are dying. A lot of my friends left me because I was too "Jesus-y" for their taste.

To this day, I still ache for them and pray for them. I try to connect with them, but mostly I get silence.

Thankfully, as all my old friends were pushing me away, those youth group kids, who had initially seemed so weird to me, were stepping in. When I would get in another disagreement with my old friends, they were there to comfort me and give me advice.

I now consider the students in the youth group some of my closest friends. Having other Christians to encourage you, love you and keep you accountable is incredibly important. When I have a question, I know I can talk to the youth pastor or one of the students. When I'm struggling, I know I can turn to them for support. And they know they can do the same with me. It's like a web, with every strand connected to other ones, so that as a whole we can reflect God's grace and truth in each other's lives.

God never meant for us to be alone. There are dozens of times in the Bible where He called His people to stand together so that no one would fall. When you're alone, that's when you start getting into trouble. If you're struggling, get plugged in to your youth group. Find someone who can keep you accountable. And TALK with them. Give them your number. They'll provide a listening ear for you, and you'll provide the same for them.

I've noticed that you tend to grow closer to both God and other Christians when you do this. You're not an island.

Maybe you don't want to bug people with your problems. Or you feel like your problems are too insignificant for other people to worry about. I'm here to tell you that you're wrong. Once you became a Christian, you've gained an entire family. Dozens of brothers and sisters. That means that when you have a problem, you can turn to them, and they'll be more than happy to come alongside you and help you because of that relationship.

James 5:13-16 talks about how we are to hurt together and rejoice together. As a Christian, you get to do that! You don't have to fight alone. Don't try. It'll bring more harm to you if you try and conceal your problems than if you tell others.

For the rest of my first year as a believer, I tried to learn as much about God as I possibly could. I fell deeper in love with Him and I gained so many new friends as a result. I had my struggles and problems, but God got me through. My relationship with Jesus grew stronger. It was wonderful!

The next year, God challenged me again at the Dare 2 Share conference. I remember the focus being on evangelism (I'm sure the focus was evangelism the preceding year, but I was otherwise occupied.) I had already realized that my friends needed to know about Jesus. After all, whenever they would listen, I had been telling them all about Him for a year. But what I hadn't realized was that there were hundreds of other people who needed to know about God, and I had the ability to tell them!

That was a stretch for me. I'm naturally very introverted. I don't like talking to strangers. It's really not my thing. So I knew that if I was supposed to tell ANYONE about God, God would have to be the one who would enable me to do that.

Maybe you're a lot like me. It's hard for you to start random conversations. You know that feeling? It's very uncomfortable for me. But here's the thing: the very essence of Christianity is uncomfortable. Take Jesus, for example: He was nailed on a cross. To call that uncomfortable would be an understatement, to say the least.

And then Jesus says things like, "Die to yourself, live for Me," and whatnot. Just check these verses out and you'll get the picture.

> Then he said to the crowd, "If any of you wants to be my follower, you must turn from your selfish ways, take up your cross daily, and follow me (Luke 9:23).

> I tell you the truth, unless a kernel of wheat is planted in the soil and dies, it remains alone. But its death will produce many new kernels—a plentiful harvest of new lives (John 12:24).

> If you refuse to take up your cross and follow me, you are not worthy of being mine (Matthew 10:38).

It's uncomfortable. Giving up the cushy, familiar things of this world in pursuit of God is uncomfortable. But Jesus decided that the crucifixion was worth the "uncomfortableness," because of what was to be gained. He tells me that dying to myself is worth the "uncomfortableness" for the same reason, and He wants me to tell other people about the God who loves them no matter who they are or where they've been.

So I asked God to give me courage and boldness. The thing about God is that He'll give you whatever you ask for. If it fits into His plans. That doesn't mean that God'll give you a smoking hot spouse, a Lamborghini, and all the money in the world just because you ask Him. But you ask God to give you the courage to share His message of grace and hope? How could He say no to that?!

So anyway, I asked God to help me tell others about Him. And guys, I tell you what. It worked!

The first person I really talked to was a waitress at a Chinese restaurant. She couldn't speak English very well, but I told her how she was loved by a holy God who wanted to take her to heaven. It was a short conversation, and I don't know how God used it, but it was the first time I had ever actually talked to someone I didn't know very well about Jesus. It was weird.

Then there was an older guy in line at Wal-Mart.

The line was ENORMOUS so we had a good, long time to discuss Jesus. I can't remember for the life of me what his name was, but he had a lot of questions, and I could tell that our conversation got him thinking.

I live in an area where there are a lot of Mormons and Jehovah's Witnesses. I've had the privilege of talking to their missionaries on many occasions.

I'm not telling you any of this to brag on myself, or anything close to that. I'm telling you this because I am SO SURPRISED that any of the conversations happened. I REALLY don't much like talking to people I don't already know. I'm awkward and weird and I tend to be very blunt. I rarely build up to evangelism. I more often than not take a very point blank approach: "Hey. Who is Jesus to you?" Or "What do you believe about God?" or "I'll never see you again, so I'm going to ask you if you have any religious beliefs. What are they?"

And initiating those kinds of questions is SO FAR out of my personality, it's not even funny. But that's what God does. He takes certain parts of our personalities and turns them upside down, so that everyone can see how mighty He is.

But in some ways, it's also hard for me to share Jesus' message with those I know personally. If I mess up and stutter in front of a stranger, or suddenly forget how to speak English, that's not ideal. But hey, if I mess up, I don't have to worry about a stranger poking fun at me the next time we cross paths. But with my friends, I just don't want to say the wrong thing, or not have the right answer!

Still, God made one donkey talk in the Bible. Apparently He's willing to use another one like me to show His awesomeness, as well, because I've had the chance to see God use some of my conversations with friends.

Let me tell you, there's no better feeling in the world than when God uses you to introduce someone to Jesus! I got to pray with a close friend of mine to accept Christ, and since she became a believer, she's been sharing her faith with her coworkers and friends! She's prayed with one of HER friends to accept Christ, and now they're working together to hit their school up for Jesus!

I got to pray with another friend, and now she's leading Bible studies at her university!

And yet a third friend is working in a homeless ministry in his church, and working with the teens there!

As a teenager, you have an awesome platform! You are in classes, art clubs, sports teams, theatre, and a hundred other places with friends who value what you have to say. You have literally hundreds of people who know you, through Facebook, Twitter, and Tumblr, who'll pay attention when you say something. Think about it: if you recommend a new band to a friend, they'll go on YouTube and listen to them, right? If you talk about Jesus to a friend, and show them that you're legitimately excited and into God, they'll be willing to listen to that as well! Maybe not all the time, but if you're passionate about God, you'll be able to share Him with your friends. He's much more important than your favorite bands, books, TV shows and movies, and you freely share those!

You have opportunities every day to tell others about God. Sometimes they're hard to see, but they're there. You may have to look outside your own personal wants or plans in order to see them. The most important thing I've learned is this: things can wait. Making dinner can wait. Cleaning up the house can wait. Even doing homework (to a certain extent) or driving home or sending an email or whatever can wait. Never rush through a conversation because you have other plans that seem more urgent or important.

You never know; maybe that person behind you in Shop-n-Save is looking for truth. You can give it to them. Could you be a few minutes late getting home? Maybe. But those few minutes could mean eternity to that person.

You may need to reprioritize your life. I'm telling

you from experience, I've wasted opportunities because I had to make a phone call, or I had to get to church on time, or I had to get home. I knew that I could have talked to someone about God, but I didn't because I didn't want to take time out of my schedule. Honestly, once I put eternity into perspective, a few minutes of my time doesn't seem like all that much.

You have opportunities **every day** *to tell others about God.*

I'm sure you've heard that saying, "I'm just a nobody who's trying to tell everybody about Somebody who can save anybody." I agree 100%. As a Christian, you are in the unique situation of being like a fire.

No, I'm not a pyromaniac at all.

But listen to me. Where I live, there are a lot of trees. Like, A TON. So every fall, we get inches of leaves the way Minnesota gets inches of snow. And the way we get rid of them is by burning the leaves. My dad was always the one who insisted on burning the leaves (because apparently, burning leaves is a manly thing to do, akin to building dog houses out of wood, fixing bathrooms and watching football). When it came time to burn the leaves, he would take all the leaves in the yard, scoop them all into a big pile, and then he'd go get one match. Now, this pile of leaves is easily four and a half feet in diameter and a good three feet high. It's a *big* pile. You really think that a tiny, two and a half inch match is going to make a difference in this huge mass of crackly, dry, brown things?

Then he would light the match and throw it into the pile. The flame would go slowly at first, barely licking the edges of the first leaf. For a minute, you'd worry that it would die out completely. And then the first leaf would catch. The heat would eat away at the dead thing, the glowing edges moving slowly up and consuming it in its entirety. The fire would then move to the next leaf, and the next, and it would continue growing from smoldering embers to a raging blaze, eventually consuming the whole heap in flames.

If you didn't know what a match did, and all you saw was this little pale twig with a bright red lump on the end, you would have never guessed the power that hid under the surface. And in reality, the power doesn't even belong to the match. The match itself can't set fire to anything. It was only when it was acted upon by an outside force and given the ability to burn that the match became useful.

And yet, it was the match that was used to make a difference. That's like us. We have no power within ourselves, but God can use us to change the world. That change starts with you.

What on Earth Was God Thinking?

That summer I experienced my first mission trip. My pastor took the youth group to Indiana to do some roofing work. It was one of the hottest weeks of the summer. I remember it literally being so hot that as we ripped the old shingles off the roof, the tar underneath re-melted and stuck to our jeans. Seriously, I am not making this up.

It was hot. Sweaty. Nasty. Dirty. And all together pretty stinkin' awesome.

Like I said, that was my first real exposure to actual mission work. For a week, my youth group and I served God and people and it was amazing. We, as people, are very tangible creatures. It's far easier for us to understand something if we can see it demonstrated before our very eyes. We see this in the gospels, when Jesus would care for someone's physical need and then minister to their spiritual need.

When we were doing the roof work, we were getting to show people God's provision in a very tangible way. God was letting us be His hands and feet. Not only were we able to show God's physical provision, but we also got to share His eternal provisions. We talked to countless people about God—how He cared for their physical and spiritual needs, and how He loved them. What we were doing had eternal value. Not because we, as people, were particularly spectacular, but because God was choosing to use us for HIS Kingdom!

That was a big thing for me. I'm a nobody, from the middle of nowhere. But God was still using someone like me for His purposes! God was changing the world (one person at a time), and I was getting to participate! It was fantastic. I knew that this was what I wanted to do with my life.

When I got home, I announced to my family that I was supposed to be a missionary, and that I was ready to sell all my belongings and live as a nomad. My parents quickly told me that no 15-year-old could do that. (Understandable.) They urged me to pray it over and then see what God was calling me to. So pray I did.

For weeks I prayed and prayed, pleading that God

would tell me how He wanted me to serve Him. I began asking my pastor, my youth pastor, ministry leaders, and basically anyone else who would listen, if they knew of any opportunities for a fiery teenager.

Eventually my youth pastor told me about this little mission group called iSalt. He had worked with one of their alumni and thought that the iSalt team might be something I should look at. So when I got home, I googled them and checked out their website.

They sounded pretty cool. The pictures were sweet. But there was a catch; it wasn't a regular mission thing. The iSalt program was a "leadership training program." The site described it this way:

> iSalt is a leadership development and discipleship program that aims to teach students and adults to view the world around them as a mission field. The program includes sixteen weeks of training and preparation, and ends with an international mission trip where the teams put what they've learned into practice.

That "international mission trip" wasn't some little weeklong stint in Mexico. I could have done that, no problem. I've seen Dora, I know basic Spanish phrases and Mexico is still on this continent. But no. The "international mission trip" that iSalt goes on is a three week jaunt to a little country called Bulgaria.

Have you even heard of Bulgaria? Yeah... I hadn't really either. I knew of its existence, but I couldn't tell you a single thing about it. I didn't know where it was, what language they spoke, or anything else like that. A quick Google search told me that Bulgaria is this tiny, little country in the middle of Eastern Europe. They speak Bulgarian, which uses a Cyrillic (Russian) alphabet. It was a long way from Midwestern Illinois.

But I felt like God wanted me to go. I brought it to my mom, and she told me to go ahead and apply. I sent in all my information to the team leaders, and they interviewed me. For some reason, they liked me. I got accepted to the mission team, and I began the training process.

For nearly four months, I practiced the language, spent time learning as much about Bulgaria as I could, and I asked God countless times if He was sure He wanted me to go overseas. Because we had people from all over the United States on our team, we didn't really have many team meetings. I talked with one of the girls, because she was my prayer partner, but I didn't know anyone else. As the dates for the actual trip grew closer, I grew more and more nervous. How could I, some random 16-year-old, actually go to Europe on a mission trip??

But the departure date came. I met the rest of the team in Chicago's O'Hare Airport. There were 12 of us, and I didn't know any of them well. Like I've made mention, I have a hard time with new people. I was scared out of my ever-lovin' mind.

I hugged my mom and dad goodbye, telling them that I'd be calling as soon as possible to let them know I was safe, and I walked down the terminal with the rest of the team. We waited for a couple hours and boarded the flight. As I sat there in the plane, I felt sick in the pit of my stomach. I was going to be in a completely foreign country for three weeks with a bunch of strangers. The same thoughts that I'd had a long time ago came back: I shouldn't be here. They don't want me here. I have nothing to offer. I can't do this. I don't want to do this anymore.

I was terrified. I hoped God knew what He was doing, because I sure didn't.

After about 14 hours of flying, with a brief layover in London, we arrived in Sofia, Bulgaria. We stepped off a tiny airplane into a tiny airport, to be greeted by a small group of Bulgarians. We tossed our bags in an old, beat up taxi, got in, and drove to our hostel. By the time we got our bags in and everything set, it was late evening. We called family members to let them know we were okay. We went out, grabbed some food, and then quickly came back—we were all exhausted from the travel. The team turned in fairly quickly that night. Except for me.

*I felt **sick** in the pit of my stomach.*

I couldn't believe that I was actually in Bulgaria. I was in a far-away country with complete strangers. The language was different. The food was different. Everything looked different. Everything sounded different. It even smelled different. I just wanted to go home. I wanted my mom and my dad and everything that was normal to me. What on earth was God thinking, sending me over here!?

We were in Sofia for two or three days. Nearly every second of those days I spent on the phone with my mom. I was trying to hold on to the tangible and familiar, instead of letting God work on me. But I didn't care; I still talked with my mom.

However, when we were getting ready to leave Sofia, one of the team leaders called me into the next room. She sat down on the bed opposite me and told me, "I don't want you calling your mom for the next three days. You won't be able to anyway, because we're going to an area where there's no internet, so this is great timing. But this is to grow you. Are you okay with this?"

I couldn't really say no.

I made one last phone call to my mom, explaining to her that I wouldn't be able to talk to her for a few days. It was literally one of the hardest conversations I'd ever had. Not necessarily for her, but for me.

It's always hard letting go of what's comfortable. Always. I don't care who you are. Sometimes, though, it's what's required if you want to know God more.

After I hung up the phone (and after I cried for a little bit), we got ready to leave. Half of the team was going to Gulyantsi. The other half, including me, was going to a little town in the mountains called Berkovitsa. Some of us would be working with the orphanage there, and others would be working in the social home. I went to the social home.

Let me explain what a social home is. In Bulgaria, if a person has a mental or physical disability (cerebral palsy, Down's syndrome, ADHD or anything else like that) they are sometimes abandoned by their family, because the family simply can't afford to care for them. When this happens, they are sent to social homes. No one visits the social homes. No one cares. People with disabilities, generally, are seen as outcasts.

The social home is one of my most vivid memories of the entire trip. I saw God at work in the midst of our experience there.

Our first day in Berkovitsa, we hiked one or two

*It's always hard **letting go** of what's comfortable... Sometimes, though, **it's what's required** if you want to know God more.*

miles to get up to the home. After about half an hour of walking, we reached some old rusty gates and an old, rundown, hotel-looking type of place. Six or seven different people, of different ages and different sizes ran up to the gate and began pulling on our hands, dragging us into the compound. One of the team leaders pulled me to the side and told me, "Go ahead and let them touch you. If you feel uncomfortable, let one of us know. But don't react suddenly to anything anyone does. If you're going to walk with them, let someone know." I nodded solemnly as one of the men there pulled my hand and jerked me towards a small ring of people who were staring intently at me.

Apparently, pale skin and blonde hair is not a common sight in Bulgaria. I found myself in the strange position of standing in the center of a circle of people as they poked and prodded me and pulled my hair. They took turns comparing their darker skin tone—they were mostly of Romani descent—to mine, because I'm about as pale as powdered sugar. They held their coal black hair next to my honey blonde.

After a few minutes of this, they bored of the strange white American, and wandered off to find someone else, except for one man. He took my hand and began walking with me in tow. I looked towards Natalie and indicated that I was going for a walk. She nodded as my new friend and I moved off.

He began chattering excitedly in Bulgarian, keeping a tight hold on my hand. After a few minutes, he fell silent and looked at me expectantly. Did he ask me a question? I had no clue. But I had to say something.

"I… speak… Bulgarian not… good." He laughed and nodded.

"I learn… am learning Bulgarian." He nodded enthusiastically. "Do you understand me?" I asked him.

"Da." Yes. He understood.

"What is your name?" I asked him.

"Dani," he answered.

"I'm Katie," I told him.

"Katie?" He worked his mouth around the foreign word. He flashed a gap-toothed grin towards me.

He pointed to his chest, "Dani." Then pointed to mine. "Katie?"

"Da!" I affirmed. I began pointing to various objects saying, "What's this?" to each one. He would say the Bulgarian word, and I would repeat. Every time, he would laugh like a proud teacher praising his pupil.

We walked laps around the compound, pointing at different objects and having a generally good time, holding hands the whole way.

See, the thing was, with people like Dani, no one wanted to really touch them. They were the equivalent of lepers. So for me to come in and hold Dani's hand for so long, to spend time with him, to talk with him, that was something that simply didn't happen. In that moment, I was being Jesus to Dani.

There were so many people that day that needed love. Was it uncomfortable? Yeah. Social homes in Bulgaria don't receive a lot of funding. And personal hygiene, to them, is not as important as having clean food and water. So a lot of them didn't bathe that often. I didn't really want to ask why most of the hands I held were sticky.

Some of my new friends there didn't understand personal space, so they would come and stand literally two inches from my nose. Others didn't like anyone touching them, and would throw a tantrum if you accidentally brushed against them. But still, they needed love.

Jesus has a wonderful way of loving when it isn't deserved. I know He's done it with me. He's held me when I've been my most abhorrent. And He gives me the opportunity to do the very same with strangers.

*Jesus has a **wonderful** way of loving when it isn't deserved.*

The only thing that the people in the social home wanted was to feel loved. They needed to know that they weren't forgotten, that they weren't unloved, that they weren't rejected. We spent about three hours with the people there. When the leaders announced that it was time to go, dozens of people lined up to give out hugs.

The feeling I had that day, I really can't convey in words. I think God gave me a taste of His love for them. Every person is infinitely loved by an infinite God. His love for each individual can't be contained; it spills over like a waterfall, refreshing anything upon which it happens to fall. I saw that in the social home. As I would wrap my arms around each person's neck and whisper, "I love you and Jesus loves you," their eyes would indubitably light up, like someone had just given them a million dollars.

That's mostly what I did while we were in Berkovitsa. Our team grew very close during that time, which was awesome, considering that at the beginning of the trip I didn't feel comfortable around ANY of the people. But serving together had helped us mesh. It was great.

Bragging on God

A few days later, we went to an old town called Stara Zagora, where most of our team did street evangelism and prayer walking. We had some obstacles with this, though.

In Bulgaria, any Christianity that isn't Orthodox Christianity (so…anything Catholic or Protestant) is considered a cult. That led to some interesting reactions when we would begin talking about God. On my first walk, I found a woman and asked her to help me with pronouncing some Bulgarian words. Clearly, she was not pleased with my attempts to interact with her because she abruptly turned around and walked away.

I was crushed. I had a hard enough time actually building up the courage to approach the woman.

I'm not good with talking to people; I'm much more comfortable just to stay quiet and not talk at all. For her to leave without a word to me actually knocked the wind out of me, and I was loathe to try witnessing again. But one of the girls pulled me to the side and told me not to let it get to me.

Evangelism is hard. It requires you to step outside of your comfort zone, and it forces you to get a little bit crazy. Someone IS going to reject you. It's not a matter of "if," but "when." And WHEN it happens, don't let it get you down.

You can't let fear of rejection keep you from ever sharing the gospel again. It's hard not to get discouraged, but you can't just give up. Jesus' gospel message is worth FAR more than that! And it matters for all eternity!

In 2 Corinthians 5:18-20 Paul lays out our incredibly important calling:

> *And God has given us this task of reconciling people to him. For God was in Christ, reconciling the world to himself, no longer counting people's sins against them. And he gave us this wonderful message of reconciliation. So we are Christ's ambassadors; God is making his appeal through us. We speak for Christ when we plead, "Come back to God!"*

So I kept this in mind as I went through the rest

of the trip. I got back up on the horse, so to speak, and had some AWESOME conversations with a lot of different people. I talked with an activist in a park for 45 minutes about sin and how "good" is "good enough," when it comes to getting into heaven. (It's impossible for us to be "good enough" on our own, that's why Jesus came and died for our sins.)

I read my Bible to a group of teenagers, and they helped me pronounce some of the words. Once I figured out how to say "resurrection" in Bulgarian, they asked me what "resurrection" meant and what made this Jesus so special that He could be resurrected.

Once, on a train, I sat next to a little old lady who didn't speak a word of English. But she saw the Bible in my lap, asked to read it, and together we read out of Romans for about ten minutes. I asked her some basic questions, and we talked for a little bit in complete Bulgarian until I had to get off the train. (To this day, I still don't quite know what I said... but it was mainly Bible verses, so it couldn't have been *THAT* bad. :-))

If you refuse to let your jittery inhibition get in the way of your Jesus exhibition, you'll find that God uses it. God wants people who are willing to be bold for Him. And if you're afraid that you can't be bold, ASK Him for help! At the end of Ephesians, Paul asks the church of Ephesus to pray for him, that he might be bold. The dude was IN JAIL for talking about God. And he was asking for more boldness? That's the excitement that God wants you and me to feel. In John 14:13-14, the Bible talks about how, if something is in God's will, you can ask for it and you'll receive it. That's how it is with courage. Just ask. God'll take care of the rest. He'll give you the gumption to speak and opportunities to act on that newfound fearlessness. I'm living proof of that. I would have NEVER been able to talk to anyone on my own, except for Jesus.

After a few days in Stara Zagora, we spent a couple hours on a bus travelling to a teen camp in the mountains where we'd be spending our final week of the trip.

I feel like Bulgarians aren't as concerned about safe driving as most Americans…considering our driver was spinning around hairpin curves at 120 kph (75 mph), with a sheet of rock on one side and a four-mile drop off on the other. While talking on the phone with one hand, and eating a cucumber sandwich with the other. I learned to trust God during that trip. Carrie Underwood doesn't even *begin* to understand the *meaning* of "Jesus, take the wheel."

Amazingly, we got to the site safe and sound. Basically, our host Bulgarian church friends had asked a ski resort if they could host a camp with them. And because most people don't do a lot of skiing in the middle of July, they were more than happy to let us come. Just as we got settled in, the rest of the camp kids arrived. All of us Americans were helping carry in the kids' bags, when one of the team leaders abruptly pulled me to the side and told me that I would be speaking at the youth camp that night.

"Uhm… okay... What do you want me to talk about?" I asked her.

"I want you to share your testimony."

I really didn't want to do that. I had never told anyone my testimony before, and I was nervous. Stack that on top of having to tell it in front of about a hundred kids through a translator, and I wasn't the happiest of campers in that moment. I excused myself and went up to my room to pray about it.

I asked God to give me the words to speak, and that He would be seen through me. I wrote down a few notes and headed down to the makeshift sanctuary. I felt like I was about to throw up. I shot up an angry little prayer, "Jesus, I HOPE You know what You're doing. You've got the *wrong* girl."

After fifteen minutes of the church pastor speaking, he motioned for me to come forward. I stood and shuffled up, every eye laser pointed on me. I looked towards the back, and my team leader was sitting there, giving me the thumbs up sign.

I closed my eyes, took a breath and began speaking. Every couple phrases I would have to stop to let the pastor translate from English to Bulgarian. I quickly forgot my notes and let God speak through me. After about fifteen minutes of sharing, I ended my story, and turned to go sit back down. The pastor stopped me, hugged me and kissed me on each cheek. After the sermon, a couple dozen kids came up to me and each embraced me tearfully. Several confided to me that they had been struggling with depression and self-injury, but I showed them that it does get better.

I take no credit for what happened that night. That was so outside of the realm of my personality, that it was truly only God who gave me the strength, and used my story to impact others. That being said, I think one of the reasons it was so powerful was because it was my story. Let me explain. No, there is too much. Let me sum up.

I could have spouted theology at them for an hour. I could have thrown logic at them, and tried to prove God's existence to them. I could have lectured them, and told them all about Jesus. But when you share your story, it provides a certain special, personal connection.

I love apologetics and I love science. But I've

noticed that when you try to have a scientific, logical or philosophical discussion regarding God with an unbeliever, they'll almost always try to disprove things. If you're sharing your personal story, they can't disprove it. It's YOUR story. You're the only one who has that story, and no one can say it isn't true.

Everybody's story is different. Everyone has a special, specific way in which God has wooed them, called them and changed them. I don't care if you were a drug-addicted, alcoholic prostitute who served thirteen years in jail for murdering your pimp before you found Jesus. I don't care if you went to church nine months before you were born, were weaned on communion wafers and grape juice and had the entire book of Leviticus memorized before you found Jesus. Your story is *your story*, and God will use your story for His purpose.

*Your story is **your story**, and God will use your story for His purpose.*

Like I've made mention, I didn't grow up in church. So my testimony may not strike as strong a chord with someone who packed out their Awana sash as a child. However, my best friend grew up in church. So whether we come from churched or unchurched backgrounds, we have a tremendous bond in Christ. Her story will speak to some people more powerfully than mine might. God uses all our stories for His glory and His kingdom purposes. And God is in the business of using and specially tailoring everyone's story—even the pain-filled and sin-soaked ones—so that each person's story may have the most possible impact for His kingdom.

That week at camp was great. All the Americans ended up sharing their testimony, and I saw the principle I just mentioned play out. Some of the kids connected with my story, while some were drawn to other's stories. And no story was made more important than any other, because every journey toward a deep, personal, trusting relationship with Jesus is a miracle.

Because no story IS more important than another. Every testimony is a retelling of God's love story. Every testimony is a wonder, of turning a dead man into a live one. Even yours. Your story is amazing! Don't try to hide it because you feel it's not special. You're a living miracle. Get out there and start bragging on the God who saved you!

Your New Song

After our team left Bulgaria and got back home, my world radically changed. I realized that the opportunities that I had in Bulgaria, I also had in the States. There was the same hurt, the same pain and the same need for God. So I figured I would start in my immediate area.

I live in Midwestern Illinois, about 45 minutes away from St. Louis. It's practically in my backyard. It's also a city with a high homeless population. I, as a 16-year-old kid, figured that I could change that. When I got home, I talked with my mom about serving the homeless. She found a church near our area that had a homeless ministry and signed us up to go. We went out with about ten other people, and started walking the streets of St. Louis, handing out clothes and food and praying with people.

Shortly after our first experience reaching out to the homeless with that other church, I talked with my mom about bringing the idea before OUR church and seeing if anyone would want to get involved in this kind of ministry. She encouraged me to organize a group. Initially, we started small— just four people handing out water bottles and ten blankets (literally). Over the months, it grew to about fifteen people, three vehicles and mounds of clothes, Bibles, blankets and homemade food for our friends on the streets.

Meeting people's physical needs is incredibly important, and I got great joy from helping the homeless, but I began to sense that God was prompting me to launch out in a new ministry direction. I felt led to start a Bible study with the youth group. So I talked with the high schoolers in the church, and invited them to meet me at McDonald's for Bible study. The first time, it was just me for a while, until a Jehovah's Witness sat down across from me and began studying the Bible with me. The next month, another girl came. Then another. Then a couple guys came. Then their parents came. Within four months, what had been just me turned into two separate studies—a student group and a women's group.

People often noticed us there in McDonald's, and some would come up and ask us questions about what we were reading. So many awesome conversations came from that, as well.

God's continued breaking me out of my introverted shell, and I can see the fruit of that: I've had countless conversations with complete strangers about the gospel. Not by my own strength, but His.

This is something I talked about earlier. Every second you are in contact with someone, there is an opportunity to share Christ. Nothing is coincidence; God Himself ordained every moment of your day and placed you exactly where you are, so that you could be a light for Him. Nothing is wasted, nothing is an accident. Don't let any opportunity pass you by.

***Nothing** is wasted, **nothing** is an accident.*

As I grow in my walk with Jesus, I'm continuing to feel God pulling me in towards Him. After much prayer, I know that God is calling me into full-time missions. I expect to mostly be serving overseas, but while I'm in the US, I'm always looking for how God wants to use me NOW. And God provides opportunities in amazing ways! I got a job at a Christian bookstore that actually pays for the employees to go on missions. How cool is that?!

Even as I'm writing this, I am astounded with how much God has worked in me. You've gotten a glimpse of the deep, dark place I used to inhabit. There was nothing I could do for myself. But God Himself reached down and pulled me up.

> *He lifted me out of the pit of despair,*
> *out of the mud and the mire.*
>
> *He set my feet on solid ground*
> *and steadied me as I walked along.*
>
> *He has given me a new song to sing,*
> *a hymn of praise to our God.*
>
> *Many will see what he has done*
> *and be amazed.*
>
> *They will put their trust in the Lord.*
>
> Psalm 40:2-3

I thank God that He saved me, and I would be perfectly content with sitting quietly in the back pew, never saying another word. But God has other plans. He's given me a new song to sing, and I simply have to sing it. And as I do, He's using me to advance His kingdom.

He's using you too. You may be just a kid. Just a high schooler with big eyes and high goals. No one may take you seriously. No one took David seriously, either. Nor Gideon. Not even Jesus was regarded as a world-changer. They crucified Him. But with God, you don't have to rely on other people's assessments of you. They don't matter. Only God's opinion of you matters.

Only God's opinion of you matters.

Ephesians 3 talks about how God can do more than anyone can possibly ask or imagine. God delights in taking you far past your hopes and dreams. He wants to take your life, shake it up, mold it, and make a new being of you. This is the God who holds nothing back from you. All He asks is that you hold nothing back from Him. He wants you to sing the new song He's given you.

I can't wait to see what He does with you.

If You or Your Friends Are Struggling

If you or your friends are struggling with self-injury, depression or suicidal thoughts, or are dealing with the aftermath of sexual abuse, please find someone you trust and talk to them about it. Share the details and let them assist you in finding help.

Don't struggle alone, and don't beat yourself up about needing help, or worry about being judged. All of us come up against things in our lives that we can't handle on our own. It's actually a measure of great courage when you reach out to get help for yourself or for someone you care about.

Connecting with your youth leader is good place to start, or talk to a trusted teacher or counselor at your school. They can assist you in finding the help you need locally in your own community.

If you aren't comfortable with confiding in someone you know personally, call one of the hotlines on the next page or visit these websites. They'll connect you with people who are trained to help.

My Broken Palace

www.mybrokenpalace.com

Dawson McAllister Hopeline

1-800-394-HOPE (1-800-394-4673) or
www.thehopeline.com/getHelp

Self-Injury Outreach and Support

sioutreach.org/

National Suicide Prevention Lifeline

1-800-273-TALK or
www.suicidepreventionlifeline.org/gethelp

God wants to replace the lies and darkness bombarding you with the truth of His light. You are not worthless—God views you as precious. You are not unlovable—God loves you so much that He sent His son Jesus to die on the cross for you, so that you might put your trust in Him and enter into a personal, restored relationship with Him! To learn more about Jesus' gift of hope and grace, go to somethingamazing.net.

Jesus came to set the captives free. So reach out, get help and let God's truth break the chains that are holding you captive.

Acknowledgments

For my entire life, I wanted to be a writer. Getting this book published has been such a wonderful experience, and I just wanted to take a quick second to give thanks where it's due.

Above all, this book is the handiwork of God. He gave me a story and a future, and He's still upholding me. Apparently, He's still in the business of bringing dead people back to life. Soli Deo Gloria!

All the Dare 2 Share people—thank you first for following God and preaching His word to so many students and being a catalyst for the movement of God in my generation, and also for giving me this opportunity. Y'all are pretty awesome.

The editor, Ms. Jane Dratz, thank you for all your patience and wisdom! I literally have NO clue how this could have even gotten off the ground without you. Thank you so much!

Shout out to my family for putting up with me for the past two decades and all the craziness that has ensued. It's been hard, but we're still making it. :-) I'm so thankful for you all. I love you!

To my friends who've stood by and provided the encouragement I needed at the right moments. You have no idea what that's meant to me. Thank you.

Thanks to the guy that made the internet—without e-mail, I'm not sure how any of this could have even ever happened.

And then, to you. Thank you for picking up this little book. Thank you for pursuing God, thank you for living for Him. I pray for you daily. May God bless you and protect you, and may He be gracious towards you and give you peace.

MORE FROM DARE 2 SHARE

These and other great resources available at www.dare2share.org

INZANE

by Zane Black

Zane's life story will inspire you to live for Christ! Told in his raw, honest, conversational style, *InZane...Totally Stoked on this Jesus Dude* captures Zane's journey from a party boy to a committed Christian. His story will keep you turning the page, and at the same time challenge you to put Jesus at the center of your life.

RECKLESS

Following Jesus to the Point of No Return

by Zane Black

Zane's casual style draws you in as he explores what being a fully committed Jesus follower looks like. He'll challenge you to personally and practically respond to Jesus' invitation to *"Come, follow me...and I will make you fishers of men."*

DARE 2 SHARE CONFERENCES

Join us at Dare 2 Share's weekend student evangelism training conferences and be equipped to share your faith. Current events schedule available at
dare2share.org/conferences